HIGH SCHOOL IS OVER

Advice for Life After Graduation

I am proud to be a high school teacher
who works with students like you.
I've taught Engineering and Design since 2015.
Before that, I worked as an adolescent
counselor and then
I taught psychology for 15 years.

One thing I learned in my experience is this:
"The worst vice is advice"
and yet, because you are a special
person and I care about your future, I am
going to break my own advice to
give a little to you.
Take it with a grain of salt but at
least consider what I have to say.
After all, I am an old man and old men
are wise, or at least supposed to be.

I suggest you only read one or two pages per
day and really put some thought into them.
Some things are very simple yet profound.

Integrity is EVERYTHING!

Live your life how you see fit. Just
understand that _everything you do_, effects
everyone around you ... and, as scary
as it sounds,_ everything you don't do_
effects everyone just as much.

For God's sake man ...

"Your garbage goes in the garbage can people. I can't stress that enough." - The Simpsons

If you want people to trust you,
they may expect you to be trustworthy.

If you are going to be embarrassed
to talk about it later, don't do it now!

People wonder what the meaning of life is.
In other words, "does life have meaning?"
My belief is that you have been given the
responsibility to create meaning in your
life. That's a big responsibility.
Don't worry, if you fail you'll just
will die inherently miserable and
unfulfilled.

So, what meaningful pursuits will you
dedicate your life to?

For all of you living in a dorm or an apartment complex with pre-pay laundry equipment... Make friends with someone that rents a house - a house that has its own washer and dryer.

"It's what you learn AFTER you know everything that counts." - John Wooden

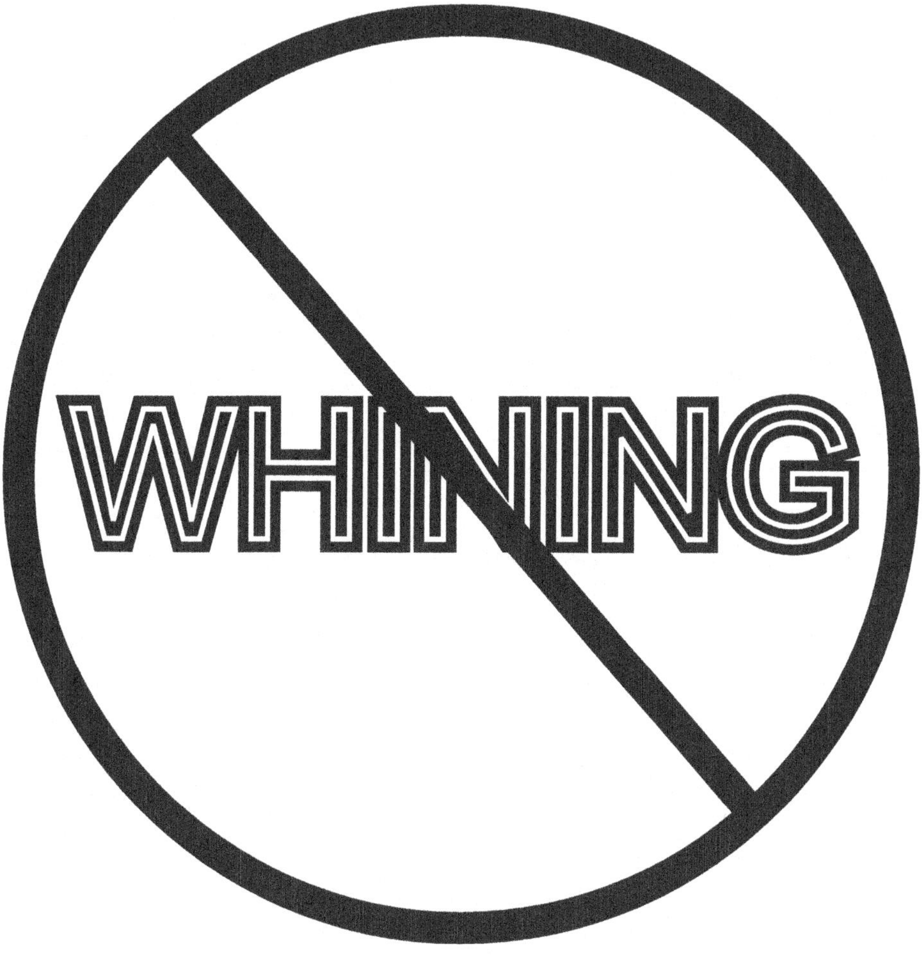
WHINING

"The easier it is to be good,
the harder it is to be GREAT." - Bob Moawad

Think about why that might be.

If you are going to drink to socialize, drink light beer. Light beer has less alcohol than other drinks. Less alcohol = less damage. You'll still fit in the crowd and you won't do something stupid if you just nurse a couple light beers. Shots ... yeah, they don't work that way.

Stay in a group of trusted friends.

(Seriously, don't move on in this book until you have examined the importance of this one sentence).

If you want to come up with good ideas, you need to come up with a whole bunch of ideas ... your first ideas are rarely the best ones.

"What luck for rulers that men do not think." - Adolf Hitler

Think hard about that one, who said it, and how to not be one of the people he's talking about.

Everything in MODERATION.
Stay in control.
Sometimes when you start to lose
control, you don't know it.

List all the things that you can truly control.

Go ahead and do it here ... the bottom
of this page is more than enough room.

If the person you are dating is an
asshole to the waiter, they are
an asshole period.
Believe it or not, it is a
matter of time before
they treat you the same way.
Get rid of them.

Don't marry someone because
they are "fun". Fun runs out.
Look for three things in a long term relationship:
1. Is this a good person that I can
respect morally and ethically?
2. Does this person respect me?
3. Would I want my future children
to be married to someone exactly like this
(if they aren't good enough for the ones
you love, they aren't good enough for you)

liquor before beer, you're in the clear
beer before liquor, never sicker

or

beer before hard, go puke in the yard

KEEP YOUR PRIORITIES IN MIND!

Make sure your behaviors
support your priorities

Is what you are doing moving you
closer or further from your <u>prioritized</u> goal?

You can't put a foot in a shut mouth

Go to class.
It's the reason you are in college

-Or-

go to work

Neither of those involve the
saying, "I don't feel like it today."

"The 'good things' in life can be the mortal enemies of the 'great things'"- Bob Moawad

or

The good life kills the great life

(Think hard about what that means)

"One of the greatest pain to human nature
is the pain of a new idea." - Walter Bagehot

(I taught entire courses of
Psychology focusing on that
one single point)

They say that this is the most exciting
time of your life, enjoy every minute of it.

Just don't trade
your self-respect for a good time.

Be kind, respect others, and think for yourself. The person you develop into now will be who you are from now on.

Clean your bathroom regularly.
It will develop fungus.

(I think they may have spray and
walkaway
shower cleaner)

The only way to create new ideas is to be unafraid of failure. When you learn from every failure, those failures become stepping stones to success.

Bring your character and integrity with you everywhere you go. If you don't, you may lose them and never find them again.

Having people to go to for support when you need it = HEALTHY

Expecting people to fulfill your needs = JACKASSERY

"What you do speaks so loud, I can't hear a word you say" - Ralph Waldo Emerson

Think about that when you are looking for a spouse... They should be thinking about that when looking for you.

Work Hard and Take Pride in what you do.
Lazieness and selfishness are
the worst human characteristics.
Avoid them at all costs

Control what you are responsible for controling.

Adjust to everything else.

Put effort into everything you do.

Many people are irresponsible. Don't let
their attitudes make you feel that you
are in the wrong by trying to be a
healthy, responsible person. Undisciplined,
irresponsible people will do anything to
pull you into their chaos.

"The great masses of people ...
will more easily fall victims to a great
lie than to a small one".- Joseph Goebbels / Adolf Hitler

If you tell a lie big enough and keep
repeating it, people eventually will
come to believe it." - Joseph Goebbels / Adolf Hitler

Lying, psychopathic bastards....
We can often learn a lot from people we want
to be nothing like... such as the necessity
of thinking for yourself and challenging
status quo thoughts.

Remember that cocky, self-agrandizing know-it-all that everyone liked and wanted to spend time with?

Neither do I.

You didn't get to where you are by yourself. Someone had to help you. Maybe you ought to thank some of those people.

Every now and then, step back and
think about your priorities.

Then, consider the things you spend the
most time doing - because those
things are your real priorities.

If you aren't comfortable with that,
find better ways to spend your time.

Any time you feel that you absolutely
need a drink, that is when you
absolutely should find a different
way to cope...unless developing
an addiction is on your bucket list.

If you are not ready to be a parent,
don't do anything that could
make you a parent.

Wear flip-flops to the shower. It's where your roommate pees.

The key to happiness:
work and love - Sigmund Freud

Be the kind of person with whom you
would like to have a relationship

The chlamydia you get in Las Vegas
does <u>not</u> stay in Las Vegas

Fostering healthy relationships is
as important as any college education ...
actually, far more important.

"Be more concerned with your character than your reputation. Your character is who you are. Your reputation is merely what people think you are"- John Wooden

Its ok to wear the same pair of pants a few times without washing them.

"How you do anything is how you do everything." - Martha Beck

Take pride in what you do ... everything you do.

Surround yourself with people that
will help you improve as a person

"Life is hard.
It's harder if you're stupid" - John Wayne

A winner makes commitments.
A loser makes promises.

A winner will get things done.
A loser will "try".

A winner says, "how might I...".
A loser says, "it's impossible."

A winner faces difficult problems
and seeks solutions.
A loser goes around problems and avoids
the pain they present.

A winner strives to be the best they can be.
A loser wants other people to think they are
the best even though they are not.

-Adapted from the University of West Virginia Football

A winner honestly assesses one's self constantly.
A loser is consumed by what others might think.

winner is not afraid to fail and learn from it.
A loser avoids the possibility of failure and
therefore, stays stagnant.

A winner knows that the truth is more important
than their beliefs and therefore, self-evaluates.
A loser looks only at those things that support
what they already want to believe.

A winner is a giver.
A loser is a taker.

A winner cares about others.
A loser puts themselves first.

-Adapted from the University of West Virginia Football

If you have sex with someone that is
intoxicated, you can be tried
and convicted for rape. No joke.

Don't get marrried or engaged while in college ... and for God's sake, don't move in together - playing house is just a bad idea no matter how great you think it will be.

Deep seated, unconscious anger is
typically the cause of self-sabotage.
If you want to be emotionally healthy,
you have to work to forgive - to truly forgive.

Forgiveness is about letting go
of your anger.
Remember, forgiveness doesn't mean
you are ok with their behavior, it doesn't
mean you have to be their friend or hang out.
It just means you let go of the anger.
Forgiveness is for you.
Trust is for them. You can forgive, but
you might never trust them again.

Be aware of your surroundings.
Stupid people
can lurk in the safest places

Some questions to ask at the beginning of
a relationship:
1. Do you like Italian food?
2. What's your favorite color?
3. Are you a borderline-personality-disorder?
(Google It!)

Anti-socials
will just use you, steal your money,
and try to kill you.
Borderlines, Narcissists, and Histrionics
will burrow into every crevice of your life
and feed on your soul - learn what to look
for and avoid them at all costs!!

#1 red flag = selfishness and entitlement

Don't form relationships with people who are selfish.

Takers just take - (I'm surprised I have to say that. I mean it is literally IN the term "takers")

Don't drink/use and drive.

PERSEVERE ... the way
we deal with adversity defines our
true character.

Every illicit drug effects your judgement.
Therefore, you can't effectively evaluate
how stupid or impaired you are when using.

It's one of the universes greatest jokes on us.

Don't hang out with jackasses

Love is about helping another person grow
It's not about obedience. It's not about control.
It's not about trying to make someone happy
all the time, doing what they want you
to do or saying what they want you to say. It is
about caring, supporting and encouraging growth,
and doing what is best for them.
If you're in a relationship,
understand what love really looks like.

The ability to delay gratification is
the cornerstone of self-discipline

Body spray is not the same as a shower.

You're not in middle school anymore but you should still know that if you get in a fist fight with someone - you hit them, they hit their head on the ground and die, you go to prison for manslaughter. It's called a "one-punch homicide". A judge told me that ... I'll let you figure out the situation that led her to tell me.

Don't use your roommates soap.
"Think of the last place I wash and the
first place you wash." - Joey Tribbiani from Friends

It is tough to get along with roommates. Like all relationships, be up-front and honest when there is conflict. Don't let things fester - instead respectfully share your conflict so it is in the open and you can work to find a solution. Be honest about the small stuff _before_ it becomes big stuff

Nobody "makes" you mad. Nobody "makes" you happy. You and you alone are in control of your level of happiness. It is one of the few things you can control.

Focus on what you want,
not what you want to avoid

Perception determines reality.
You can control your perception.

The key to mental health is
to pursue reality at all costs - especially
when it conflicts with your current
beliefs. - M. Scott Peck

(Don't know M. Scott Peck? You need to
read "The Road Less Traveled"! Then
read it again...and again.)

"You are, you become, you act like, and you move toward what you think about." - Lee Hitchcock, wise old man

What are you thinking about?

Think positive and seek solutions

A positive attitude is critical!

"You can't solve a problem by saying it is someone else's problem." - M. Scott Peck

Who is responsible for that?

Take responsibility for the things
you can control.

A friend will tell you when you have
a bugger on your lip

Always keep one clean shirt in the closet
for emergencies even if you have to
wear a dirty shirt when it's not critical.

Some people care about you enough
to tell you to pull your head out of your ass.
As John Wooden said "surround yourself
with smart people that are willing to
argue with you"

Want a novel solution?
Come up with wild ideas that seem impossible,
ask "yes, and", and work them into
real solutions for real people,
make millions of dollars.

Ever hear someone say, "I drive
better drunk because I'm more careful"
. . .yup, they are idiots.

"Noone can make you feel inferior without your consent" - Eleanor Roosevelt

Take risks.
I knew a guy in high school
who started a company networking
computers together. We could invest
for $1,000. That's crazy. No college student
just has $1,000 sitting around to risk.

Of course, it wasn't so crazy when he sold
his product "photo-bucket" to MySpace
(popular social media site before Facebook).
Oh, I forgot to mention the buying price was
$330 million dollars - split between him and
only one other guy.

There are people who listen and people who just wait to talk - nobody respects the second group.

Trust is fragile. It is easy to destroy
and nearly impossible to rebuild.

One of the most powerful ways to show you care about someone is simply to listen to them

THC is absorbed in body fat - and it stays there for years! The fattiest area of the body is the brain. The second fattiest area of the body are the reproductive organs.

Have you ever been annoyed because
you knew you were right about something
but other people just wouldn't listen?

I hate that!

I hate it even worse when I find out three
days later that I was actually wrong.

I guess I didn't know after
all ... you ever done that?

Condoms are far from 100% effective.
Just thought you ought to know that.

Average people pass out from alcohol at a
BAC of .35%
50% of people die when BAC reaches .4%
When a person is passed out, their body is still
absorbing the contents in their intestines.
Puking does not purge the intestines.
Therefore, if you see someone passed out, they
have about a 30-40% chance of reaching a
lethal level of alcohol poisoning.
Don't draw on their face and shave their eyebrows
- instead, call 911.
Legally, you can't be ticketed for doing so. You
can be charged for doing nothing.

Don't let your friends leave a party with people they don't know or you don't trust.

THC is an insidious chemical. It settles in
your brain and causes progressive and
chronic slowing of neural functioning.
In layman's terms - it slowly makes you stupid

Additionally, THC stays in the body for years
- even decades after use has stopped.

Know you're good and wear it well.
Confidence is attractive.
Arrogance is repulsive.

Don't ever throw a college party with alcohol or drugs. There are plenty of parties out there without yours.
If someone gets hurt at
your party, you can
end up sued or in prison.
It has happened often...actually kind
of a regular thing.

THC is a safe drug - FALSE
THC is not addictive - FALSE
THC is less damaging than alcohol -FALSE

It is highly carcinogenic, has basically the same neural mechanism of action as heroin, and shuts down neural functioning by blocking neural pathways which can last for years

Don't procrastinate.
Despite what you want to believe,
you really do not work
better under pressure.

Trust is expensive. It usually costs
years of consistent honesty and integrity.

Simple math:
$$x + y = z$$

x = healthy relationships
y = meaningful accomplishments
z = fulfillment

After you proof read your papers,
proof read them again from back to front.

With all the great things you are about to accomplish, it may be difficult to act humble as opposed to cocky.

Whatever you do today,
you have to sleep with from now on.

Intelligence may get you hired, but it is your personality and empathy that gets you promoted.

Keep Perspective
Although life can seem impossible at times,
reality is that if this page were the Earth,
your problems
would rarely be as large of the period
at the end of this sentence.

Don't confuse fun and excitement
with happiness and fulfillment.

Let me say that again ...

Don't confuse fun and excitement
with happiness and fulfillment.

WHO IS RESPONSIBLE FOR YOUR
CHOICES AND BEHAVIORS?

- There is only one right answer to
that question every single time!

"The best day of your life is the one on which you decide your life is your own. No apologies or excuses. No one to lean on, rely on, or blame. The gift is yours - it is an amazing journey - and you alone are responsible for the quality of it. This is the day your life really begins." - Bob Moawad

I want you to know that
I have no doubts that
you can make this world
a better place.

I thank you in advance
for doing that.

Made in the USA
Coppell, TX
04 June 2023